Boggle Me Brain!

Fun Word Games for Young Geniuses

(Ages 10 and Up)

Boggle is a timed word-search game for two or more players.

<u>To play</u>

Once the Big Boggle grid is randomized a **three-minute timer** is started and all players simultaneously begin the main search-phase of play.

Players must visually string together adjacent letters in the correct order to create a word (**This edition 4- to 5-letter words**). Adjacent letters neighbor each other horizontally, vertically, or diagonally.

Each player records all the words found by writing on a private sheet of paper.

After three minutes have elapsed, all players must immediately stop writing. The game now enters the scoring phase.

Word Letter Count	4	5
Word Score	1	3

I	E	D	O	Qu
D	O	V	E	C
D	A	R	I	E
L	T	R	R	E
E	N	N	A	A

Score

Word Letter Count	4	5
Word Score	1	3

E	I	E	P	N
S	F	L	H	L
A	P	E	V	A
T	O	A	N	X
S	W	I	E	M

Word Letter Count	4	5
Word Score	1	3

N	U	O	A	I
R	D	T	R	E
P	J	T	C	E
E	D	E	L	S
E	L	F	R	R

Score

Word Letter Count	4	5
Word Score	1	3

E	I	I	R	D
I	S	Z	R	L
O	E	S	L	E
D	N	M	O	L
A	D	R	A	H

Score

Word Letter Count	4	5
Word Score	1	3

N	L	Z	I	N
E	E	E	E	A
Y	H	O	U	I
C	R	I	C	G
P	F	E	D	S

Score

Word Letter Count	4	5
Word Score	1	3

E	U	Z	S	O
R	H	E	L	E
T	T	A	N	R
T	S	D	N	O
S	Y	A	S	E

Score

Word Letter Count	4	5
Word Score	1	3

D	A	M	O	T
P	O	T	T	S
I	I	N	R	A
R	W	S	R	A
Qu	S	A	T	D

Score

Word Letter Count	4	5
Word Score	1	3

H A	T	E	E
O	S	T	A	E
Qu	G	F	U	E
R	H	D	T	I
I	N	G	P	P

Score

Word Letter Count	4	5
Word Score	1	3

N	T	T	B	A
O	H	U	A	E
C	S	E	E	T
I	E	T	R	A
S	Y	R	N	E

Score

Word Letter Count	4	5
Word Score	1	3

R	E	O	M	H
N	R	E	A	O
T	R	T	E	P
R	N	T	I	U
E	N	X	P	S

Score

1

VIREO
VIRED
VIRAL
VICED
VERRA
VARNA
VAREC
VARAN
VALET
VADED
TROVE
TRODE
TROAD
TRIER
TRIED
TRICE
TRAVE
TRADE
TAVER
TARRE
TARED
ROVED
RODEO
RODED
ROATE
RIVER
RIVED
RIVAL
RIEVE

RICER
RICED
REVIE
REIVE
REEVE
REEDE
REDED
RAVER
RAVED
RATEL
RAREE
RARED
RADIO
QUEER
OVOID
OVERT
OVATE
ORVAL
ORATE
OATEN
OARED
NARRE
NARIC
LAVER
LAVED
LATEN
LAREE
LADED
IRATE
IRADE
EVERT
EVADE
ERRED
ERODE

EERIE
DOVIE
DOVER
DOVED
DORIC
DOREE
DORAD
DIODE
DERAT
DEICE
DEERE
DEDAL
DARRE
DARIC
DARED
COVER
COVED
CODER
CODED
CEDED
AVOID
AVERT
ARTEL
ARTAL
AROID
AREIC
AREDE
AREAR
ANTRE
ANTRA
ANTAR
AERIE
ADORE
ADDLE

ADDIO
ADDED
VOID
VOAR
VIRE
VIER
VIED
VICE
VERT
VERA
VEER
VARE
VARA
VALE
VADE
TROD
TRIE
TREE
TRAD
TELD
TELA
TARO
TARN
TARE
TARA
TALE
ROVE
ROED
RODE
ROAR
ROAD
RIVO
RIVE
RIVA

RICE
REED
REDO
REDE
REAR
REAN
RAVE
RATE
RARE
RANT
RALE
RADE
QUOD
OVER
OVAL
ORRA
ORAL
ORAD
ODOR
ODAL
NARE
LENT
LAVE
LATE
LARN
LARI
LARE
LADE
IRED
ICER
ICED
EVOE
EVER
ETNA

ERIC
EDDO
ECOD
EARN
DOVE
DORT
DORR
DORE
DOER
DODO
DOAT
DIED
DEVA
DERV
DERO
DEID
DEER
DECO
DATE
DART
DARN
DARI
DARE
DALT
DALE
DADO
COVE
COED
CODE
CIVE
CIRE
CERT
CERO
CERE

CEDE
AVER
ARVO
ARNA
ARED
AREA
ARAR
ANTE
ANTA

2

XENIA
VLIES
VLEIS
VENAL
VENAE
TWINE
TWAIN
TOWIE
TAPEN
SWOPT
SWOPS
SWINE
SWAPT
SWAPS
SWAIN
STOPS
STOPE
STOEP
STOAS
STOAI
STOAE
STAPS
SPOTS
SPEOS
SPEAN
SPAWS
SPATS
SPANE
SPAIN
SOAVE
SOAPS

SILVA	HANAP	TAOS	PANE	HEPT	**3**	OTTER	TORC
SILEN	HALVE	SWOT	PAIN	HEPS		LEEAR	TORA
SAPAN	HALVA	SWOP	OWTS	HELP		FLEER	TERF
POWIN	FLIES	SWAP	OPTS	HELE		FETTA	TELS
POWAN	FATWA	SWAN	OPEN	HEIL	UTTER	FECES	TELE
PLIES	FATSO	STOW	OATS	HEAP	URPED	ERECT	TELD
PLENA	ESILE	STOP	OAFS	HAVE	TROUT	ELFED	TECS
PLANE	ELVAN	STOA	NEPS	FLEA	TROAT	ELECT	TART
PHENE	AXMEN	STAP	NEFS	FILE	TREES	ELDER	TARO
PENIE	ASPEN	SPOT	NEAP	FENI	TREAT	EJECT	TARE
PENAL	ANELE	SPAW	NAVE	FEIS	TORTE	DOREE	SLEE
PELFS	AHEAP	SPAT	NAPS	FATS	TORES	DELES	SLED
PEISE	WOTS	SPAN	NAPE	EPOS	TORCS	CROUT	SERE
PAVEN	WOST	SPAE	NAPA	EPHA	TERSE	CREES	SERA
PAVAN	WOPS	SOPS	NAOS	EOAN	TELES	CREEL	SELF
PANEL	WINE	SOAP	NAOI	ELFS	TECTA	CERIA	SELE
PANAX	WAVE	SILE	MENE	EINE	TARES	CERES	SEER
NELIS	WAPS	SEIL	MEIN	EINA	SLEER	ARTEL	SECT
NEAPS	WANE	SEIF	MEAN	EAVE	SERAI	ARCED	RUND
NAVEL	WAIN	SAFE	LISP	AVEL	SCROD	UNDO	ROUT
NAVAL	VLEI	POWS	LIFE	AVAL	SCREE	TURN	ROTA
NAPAS	VENA	POTS	LIES	ATOP	SCRAT	TURD	REES
MEANE	VELE	POST	LIEF	APTS	SCRAE	TUND	REEL
LIFES	VAWS	POAS	LEVA	APSE	SCEAT	TROT	REDE
LIEFS	VANE	PLIE	LEPT	APOS	ROUND	TROD	RECS
LEPTA	VAIN	PLEA	LEPS	ANAL	ROTTE	TRIE	RATU
LEAPT	TWOS	PLAN	LEIS	AINE	RETRO	TRES	RATO
LEAPS	TWIN	PENI	LEAP		RELET	TREE	PELF
LANAI	TWAE	PENE	LEAN		REELS	TRAT	PELE
IOTAS	TOWS	PELF	LAVE		RECTO	TOUR	PEEL
INEPT	TOPS	PELE	LAVA		RECTA	TOUN	PEED
INAPT	TOPE	PEAN	LANX		PRUTA	TORT	OURN
HELVE	TOEA	PAWS	LANE		OUTRE	TORI	ORES
HELPS	TAPS	PAVE	LANA			TORE	ORCS
HEAPS	TAPE	PATS	IOTA				
HAVEN	TAPA	PASE	ILEA				

NURD CELT

LERE CELS

LEER CEES

LEEP CEDE

LEED ARES

JEEL ARCS

JEED AIRT

IRES AERO

FRET

FLEE

FLED

FETT

FELT

ERRS

ERES

ELSE

EELS

DURN

DOUT

DOUR

DOUN

DORT

DORE

DOAT

DELT

DELS

DELF

DELE

DEEP

CREE

CLEF

CERT

CERO

CERE

4

SORDA	NODES	HOERS	SORA	OLMS	IONS
SORAL	MOSSO	HOARD	SONS	OLLA	HOSS
SONSE	MOSES	HAROS	SONE	ODES	HOSE
SONES	MOSED	HARNS	SOME	NOSE	HORN
SONDE	MORNS	HARMS	SOMA	NOES	HORA
SOLER	MORNE	HAOLE	SOLE	NODE	HOMS
SOLAR	MORAL	HAMES	SOLA	NESS	HOME
SOLAH	MOLLS	HAMED	SODA	NEMA	HOMA
SMALL	MOLLA	HALOS	SOAR	MOSS	HOLS
SLORM	MOLAR	HALLS	SNOD	MOSE	HOLM
SIZES	MOERS	HALLO	SNED	MORN	HOLE
SIZED	MESON	HALER	SLOE	MORA	HOER
SIENS	MENAD	ERSES	SIZE	MOLS	HOAR
SEIZE	MALLS	ENROL	SIRS	MOLL	HARO
SEISE	MAHOE	ELMEN	SIRE	MOLE	HARN
SEDAN	LOSES	DROSS	SIES	MOLA	HARM
ROSES	LOSEN	DROME	SIEN	MOER	HARD
ROSED	LOSED	DROLL	SESE	MESS	HAMS
ROMEO	LORAL	DROLE	SENS	MESE	HAME
ROMAL	LOMES	DRAMS	SEND	MENO	HALO
ROLLS	LOMED	DOSES	SENA	MEND	HALL
ROAMS	LOAMS	DESSE	SEIS	MARD	HALE
RISES	LARNS	DEMOS	ROSE	MALL	ESSE
RISEN	LAMES	DADOS	ROMS	MALE	ESES
RAMEN	LAMED	AROSE	ROMA	LOSS	EONS
OMRAH	ISSEI	ARMED	ROLL	LOSE	EMOS
OMENS	HOSES	ANODE	ROLE	LORN	ELSE
OLLER	HOSEN	ANDRO	ROAM	LORD	ELMS
NOSES	HOSED	AMOLE	RISE	LOME	ELLS
NOSED	HORNS	AMENS	REOS	LOMA	DRAM
NOISE	HORME	AMEND	RAMS	LOLL	DOSS
	HORAL	ALLEL	RALE	LOAM	DOSE
	HOMES	ADMEN	OSES	LARN	DONS
	HOMED	SRIS	ORAL	LARD	DONE
	HOLMS	SORN	ONES	LAMS	DONA
	HOLLA	SORD	OMEN	LAME	DOES

DOEN
DESI
DENS
DEMO
DANS
DADO
ARNA
ARMS
ANES
AMEN
ALOE
ALLS
ADOS

5

SCOUG
SCORE
ROUEN
RICED
PRIEF
PRIED
PRIDE
PRICE
PREIF
NEEZE
NEELE
LEUCO
ICIER
HIRED
HIDER
HEEZE
GUIRO
GUIDS
GUIDE
FRIED
FIRED
FIERY
EYRIE
ERICS
DICER
DECOR
CROCS
CROCI
CRIED
CREDS
CORED

CIDER
CHORE
CHOIR
CHOCS
CHIRP
CHIRO
CHIEF
CHIDE
CHICS
CHICO
AIZLE
AINEE
ZINE
ZEIN
SCUG
ROUE
ROCS
RIFE
RIDS
RIDE
RICE
REIF
REDS
RECS
ORFE
LEHR
IRED
ICER
ICED
HYEN
HORI
HORE
HIRE
HIED
HIDE
HELE

HEEL
GUID
GUAN
GIEN
FROE
FIRE
FIER
FIDS
FICO
FICE
FEDS
EYRE
EYEN
EUOI
ERIC
EINE
EINA
DIRE
DICE
DERO
DEIF
DEFI
DECO
CUIF
CROC
CRED
CORY
CORF
CORE
COIR
COIF
CIRE
CIGS
CIDS
CIDE
CHOU

CHOC
CHID
CHIC
CHEZ
CERO
CEDI
AINE

6

ZETAS
ZEALS
TRUES
THETA
THESE
THANS
THANE
THANA
TESLA
TENOR
TENON
TENNO
TENNE
TENES
TENDS
TELOS
TELES
TEALS
TEADS
TASTY
TANNA
TANAS
TALES
TALER
TAELS
STENO
STEND
STELE
STELA

STEAN
STEAL
STEAD
STANE
STAND
STALE
SORES
SOREL
SONNE
SONES
SOLER
SOLAS
SOLAN
SOLAH
SNORE
SNATH
SLATS
SLATE
SLANE
SETTS
SETAL
SERON
SENOR
SENNA
SENDS
SENAS
SELAH
SEATS
SEANS
SAYST
SATES
SASSY
SANSA
SANES

SANER
SANDY
SANDS
SALSE
SALET
SALES
RONNE
RONES
RONEO
RHEAS
RESET
RENNE
RENDS
RENAL
RELET
ORLES
NONET
NONES
NONAS
NETTY
NETTS
NEATS
NEATH
NEALS
NATTY
NATES
NASTY
NASAL
NANAS
NADAS
LOSER
LOSEN
LETHE
LENOS

7

LENES	HAETS	TEND	SEAS	NAYS	HEAL	DAES
LENDS	HADST	TELS	SEAN	NATS	HEAD	ATES
LEATS	ETHER	TELE	SEAL	NANS	HATS	ANSA
LEAST	ETHAL	TELA	SAYS	NANE	HATE	ANON
LEANS	EROSE	TEHR	SATE	NANA	HAST	ANNS
LEADY	ERNES	TEAS	SASS	NADS	HAND	ANNO
LEADS	EORLS	TEAL	SANS	NADA	HALO	ANNA
LATHE	ENATE	TEAD	SANE	LOSE	HALE	ANES
LATEN	ELATE	TASS	SAND	LETS	HAET	ANDS
LASTS	ELANS	TANS	SALS	LENO	HAES	ANAS
LANES	ELAND	TANE	SALE	LEND	HAEN	ANAN
LANDS	EATHE	TANA	SADS	LEHR	HADS	ANAL
LANAS	EASTS	TALE	RUES	LEAT	ETHE	ALSO
HURTS	EALES	TAHR	ROSE	LEAS	ETAS	ALOE
HENNA	DATES	TAES	RONE	LEAN	EROS	ALES
HENDS	DALES	TAEL	ROES	LEAD	ERNS	
HELOS	ANNAT	TADS	RHEA	LATS	ERNE	
HELES	ANNAS	STEN	REOS	LATH	EORL	
HEATS	ANNAL	SORN	REND	LATE	EONS	
HEAST	ANELE	SORE	ORLE	LAST	ENES	
HEALS	ALOES	SONE	ORES	LASS	ENDS	
HEADY	ADAYS	SOLE	ONES	LANE	ELSE	
HEADS	ZETA	SOLA	ONER	LAND	ELAN	
HATES	ZELS	SLOE	OLES	LANA	EATS	
HASTY	ZEAS	SLAT	OLEA	LADY	EATH	
HASTE	ZEAL	SLAE	NOSE	LADS	EASY	
HANSE	YADS	SETT	NONE	HURT	EAST	
HANSA	TRUE	SETS	NONA	HUES	EANS	
HANDY	THRU	SETA	NOES	HUER	EALE	
HANDS	THEN	SENE	NETT	HETS	DAYS	
HALSE	THAT	SEND	NETS	HEND	DATE	
HALOS	THAN	SENA	NEON	HELO	DANS	
HALES	THAE	SELE	NEAT	HELE	DALS	
HALER	TENE	SEAT	NEAL	HEAT	DALE	

WRIST
WARTS
WARST
WARNS
TSARS
TRATT
TRATS
TRASS
TOPIS
TOMOS
TINTS
TARTS
TARSI
TARNS
TARAS
TAPIS
TAPIR
TAATA
SWATS
SWART
SWARD
STRAW
STRAD
STOTT
STOMA
STAWS
START
STARS
STARR
STARN
SASIN

RITTS	DRATS	TASS	PISS	DART	**8**	STAT	**9**
RAWNS	DATTO	TART	PIRS	DARN		SHOG	
RAWIN	DATOS	TARS	PION	AWNS		SHAT	
RATOS	DARTS	TARN	PINT	ATOP		SATE	
RATAS	DARNS	TARA	PINS	ATOM	TUTEE	RING	YECHS
RASTA	ATTAR	SWAT	OTTO	ATMA	TUFTS	RIND	USHER
POTTS	ATTAP	STOT	OSAR	ARTS	TEATS	PTUI	TYRES
POTTO	ARTIS	STAW	ONTO	ARTI	TAUTS	PIET	TYEES
POTIN	ARRAS	STAR	ONST	ARAR	TASTE	OATS	TUBAE
PONTS	ARARS	SRIS	OINT	APOD	STATE	OAST	TUATH
POMOS	AARTI	SOMA	NOTT		SHOAT	HOST	TSUBA
POINT	WRIT	SNOT	NOTA		INDUE	HOGS	TREYS
PITTA	WIST	SNOD	NOMA		HOSTA	HOGH	TRETS
PITON	WISS	SNIT	NOIR		HOAST	HOAS	TREST
PIONS	WINS	SNIP	NIPA		HASTE	HING	TREES
PINTS	WINO	SIRS	MOTT		HASTA	HIND	TREAT
PINTO	WATS	SIRI	MOTS		GRIND	HATS	TRANT
PINTA	WAST	SAWS	MOTI		GOATS	HATE	TOSES
PINOT	WART	SAWN	MOST		FAUTS	HAST	THOSE
PATIO	WARS	SARS	MONS		FATSO	GRIN	THETE
PATIN	WARN	SARD	MOIT		ETATS	GOSH	THESE
OTTOS	WARD	RITT	MOAT		UTAS	GOAT	THERE
OTTAR	TSAR	RIOT	MATT		TUTS	GOAS	THEES
OINTS	TRAT	RINS	IWIS		TUFT	FAUT	TETRA
NOMOS	TRAD	RAWS	IRIS		TUFA	FATS	TETES
NOMAD	TOTS	RAWN	IOTA		TETS	FATE	TERTS
NOIRS	TOST	RATS	IONS		TEAT	ETUI	TERRY
MOTTS	TOSA	RATO	INTO		TAUT	ETAT	TERRA
MOTTO	TOPI	RATA	DRAW		TATU	ETAS	TERNE
MOTIS	TONS	RAST	DRAT		TATS	EATS	TERES
MOIST	TOMO	POTT	DOPA		TATE	DUIT	TECHS
MATTS	TOAD	PONT	DONS		TASH	DUET	TAUBE
MATIN	TIPI	PONS	DOIT		TAOS	AUFS	TATUS
INTRA	TINT	POMO	DOAT		STUD	ATUA	
DRAWS	TINS	POIS	DATO		STET		
DRAWN	TAWS	PITA	DATA				

TATHS	RESET	ECHES	AREAE	TEAT	SERE	HUSO	CETE
TATER	RESES	EATHE	ANTRE	TEAR	SERA	HUES	CERT
TATAR	RESEE	EATER	ANTES	TAUT	SEIS	HUER	CEES
TARTY	RENTS	COTTA	ABUSE	TAUS	SEES	HOST	BUTT
TARTS	RENTE	COTHS	ABATE	TATU	SEER	HOSE	BUST
TARRY	REIST	COSTE	YEST	TATT	SECS	HETS	BUSH
TARRE	REEST	COSIE	YECH	TATH	SECO	HETE	BUAT
TARES	REECH	COSEY	USES	TATE	SECH	HEST	BETE
TABUS	RECON	COSET	USER	TART	SEAT	HERN	BETA
SUTTA	REATE	COSES	TYRE	TARN	SCOT	HERE	BEET
SUETY	REATA	CHUSE	TYES	TARE	RYES	HEAT	BEER
STYRE	RANTS	CHOTT	TYER	TANE	RETS	ETNA	BEAU
STYES	OTHER	CHOSE	TYEE	TAES	RETE	ETAT	BEAT
STRAE	OSIER	CHEST	TUSH	TABU	REST	ESES	BATT
STERN	OCHES	CHERT	TUBE	SYES	RESH	ERNE	BATH
STERE	OCHER	CHERE	TUBA	SUET	RENT	ERES	BATE
STEER	NOSEY	CHEER	TRYE	SUER	REIS	EISH	AUTO
STEAR	NOSES	CHEAT	TREY	SUBA	REHS	EERY	ARTY
STEAN	NOSER	CETES	TRET	STYE	REES	EECH	ARTS
SICHT	NERTS	CERTS	TRES	STEY	RECS	ECOS	ARET
SICES	NARRE	CERNE	TREE	STET	REAN	ECHT	ARES
SHOTT	NARES	BUSTY	TRAT	SOTH	RATE	ECHO	AREA
SHERE	ICHES	BUSES	TOST	SIST	RATA	ECHE	ANTS
SHEET	HOSEY	BEETS	TOSH	SIES	RANT	EAUS	ANTE
SHEER	HOSES	BEAUT	TOSE	SICS	OSES	EATH	AESC
SERRY	HOSER	BEAUS	TOCS	SICH	OCHE	EARN	ABUT
SERRE	HETES	BEATH	THUS	SICE	NOTT	COTT	ABET
SERRA	HERRY	BATTU	THON	SHUT	NOSH	COTH	
SEISE	ESTER	BATHS	THEE	SHOT	NOSE	COST	
SECHS	ESCOT	BATHE	TETS	SHET	NEAT	COSH	
REUSE	ENTRY	AUTOS	TETE	SHEA	NEAR	COSE	
RETRY	ENTER	ARRET	TERN	SEYS	NARE	CIST	
RETES	ENATE	ARETS	TEES	SETS	ICON	CHUT	
RESTY	ECHOS	ARETE	TEER	SESH	ICHS	CHUB	
			TECS	SESE	ICES	CHON	
			TECH	SERR	ICER	CHER	

UPTIE
TROAT
TREMA
TREEN
TREAT
TITRE
TITER
TERNE
TAPUS
TAPIS
TAPET
TAMER
SUITE
SPITE
SIXTE
ROATE
RETRO
RETIE
RENTE
REMAP
REATE
PUPAE
PITTA
PIPET
PIETA
PETTI
PETRE
PETIT
PETER

PATTE
PATER
OATER
MORNE
MOPUS
METRO
METRE
METIS
MERER
MATTE
MATER
MAHOE
HOMER
HATER
HAPUS
ETAPE
ENTER
EATER
AMORT
AMEER
TRET
TREE
TITE
TIPT
TIPS
TETE
TERN
TEPA
TEER
TEEN
TEEM
TEAT
TEAM
TAPU

TAPE
TAME
SUPE
SUIT
SUET
SPUE
SPIT
SPIE
SITE
SIPE
ROMA
ROAM
RETE
RENT
REEN
REAP
REAM
PUPS
PUPA
POMO
POME
POET
PITA
PIPS
PIPE
PIPA
PIET
PEER
PEAT
PATE
OPUS
OPAH
OMER
NEEM

MORT
MORN
MORE
MOPE
MOER
MOAT
METE
META
MERE
MEET
MEER
MEAT
MATT
MATE
ITEM
HOPE
HOMO
HOME
HOMA
HATE
HAPU
HAME
HAET
HAEM
ERNE
AERO